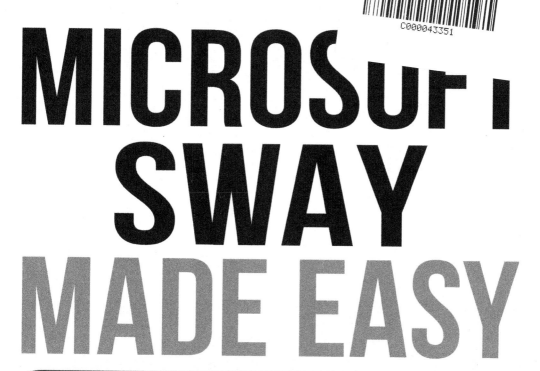

MICROSOFT SWAY
MADE EASY

Presenting Your Ideas With Style

By James Bernstein

Bernstein, James
Microsoft Sway Made Easy
Part of the Productivity Apps Made Easy series

For more information on reproducing sections of this book or sales of this book,
go to **www.madeeasybookseries.com**

Contents

Introduction

Microsoft Sway has been around for several years but has had a few updates during its lifetime. And even though it's been around for a while, many people have still never heard of it. It's similar to PowerPoint except you wouldn't really use it for presentations even though you technically can with the slide feature that comes with the app.

Sway can be used to create various document types such as flyers, interactive reports, personal stories and yes, even presentations. These documents are then referred to as "Sways". Of course it takes a little know how to add some flair to your work to really wow your audience and even that is not too difficult once you get the hang of how things work.

The goal of this book is to teach you how to get up and running with Sway and show you how all the tools and features work, so you know where you need to go to do what you need to do. I will go over how to create basic Sways as well as how to add some advanced features to them so you can make yourself look like a pro even if you might not be!

I will be using the website version of Sway even though there is a desktop client that functions exactly the same. I will show you how to install the Sway app as well in case you want to check it out.

Once you have your Sway ready to go, you can then share it with others via a link that you can email and you can even give other people access to edit your work. You can also export your work to a Word document or PDF file.

So on that note, let's get started making some eye catching Sways that will be sure to wow your audience... and maybe even yourself!

Chapter 1 – What is Microsoft Sway?

If you are like many people, you have not even heard of Microsoft Sway until you maybe stumbled across it or heard about it from someone else. Then you decided to check it out for yourself and that is what led you to read this book on how to use it!

Introduction to Sway

Sway is part of the Microsoft Office online suite of apps which includes many other apps that you might not have heard of such as Forms, Lists and Teams for example. When most people think of Microsoft Office, they are thinking of apps such as Word, Excel, PowerPoint and Outlook etc. These apps can be used online as well as via your desktop computer as installed programs.

For the most part, Sway is an online app even though there is a desktop client\app that you can install on your computer. When you use online specific apps, you can access them from any device that has an internet connection and a web browser. This way you can work on your documents etc. without having to be at home or at the office in front of your computer.

Many people like to compare Sway to PowerPoint and even though you can make a slide based presentation in Sway, they are not the same thing. PowerPoint has more advanced features and is better for the workplace while Sway might be better to use at home or at school. I like to think of Sway as being for the personal user and PowerPoint for the corporate user even though you can use either of the apps interchangeably.

Microsoft Accounts

Just like with anything tech related these days, you will need to have a Microsoft account in order to use Sway. If you are a Windows user, then you already have a Microsoft account that you use to log into your computer. If you have an Office 365 account, then once again you have a Microsoft account. Many people use the same Microsoft account to log into Windows as they do for their Office apps.

If you don't want to use your current Microsoft account for Sway or are using someone else's account to log into Windows or maybe a work account, then you can easily create a free Microsoft account online. To do so, simply navigate to the Microsoft account website from your web browser (https://signup.live.com/) and then you will be prompted to create an account with an existing email address or phone number, or you can create a new email address just for this account.

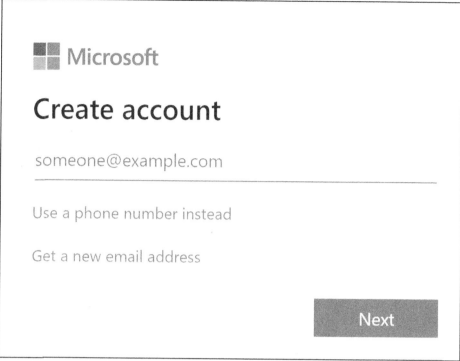

Figure 1.1

If you prefer not to have a new email address just to use for your Microsoft apps, you can type in your current email address and choose a password and use this address for your account. The password does not have to be the same as the one associated with your current email account.

If you do decide to get a new email address to use with your Microsoft account then you will need to come up with an address that is not in use by someone else and then choose if you want it to end with *outlook.com* or *hotmail.com*.

 I would suggest using an outlook.com email address since Hotmail is an older platform that Microsoft is starting to phase out in favor of Outlook accounts. If you do use or have a Hotmail account, it will most likely be transferred to an Outlook account in the future.

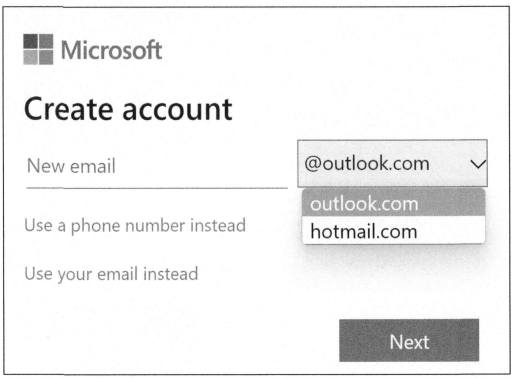

Figure 1.2

Once you have your Microsoft Account created, you can use it to log into the Sway website.

Accessing Sway
Now that you are officially part of the Microsoft family, it's time to access the Sway website to see how it looks and get an idea of what you are in for. To do so, simply go to https://sway.office.com/ or you can go to your Microsoft account at https://www.office.com/ and click on the app launcher to see all of your available apps. To get to Sway from there, you might have to click on *All apps* at the bottom of your app list.

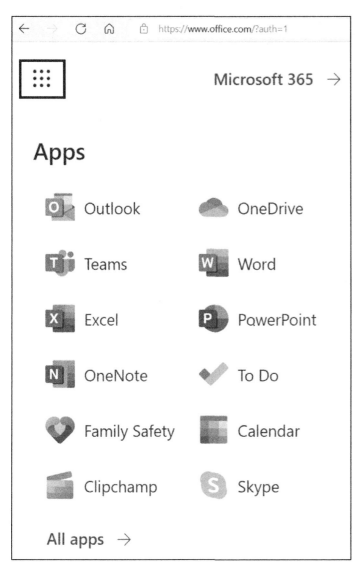

Figure 1.3

The Sway Interface

Once you access Sway for the first time, you will see that the interface is fairly simple and it doesn't look like there is a lot to it. As you can see in figure 1.4, you have a few options such as create a new Sway, start from a topic or start from an existing document. Then at the bottom, there are some templates to choose from as well as some examples you can check out.

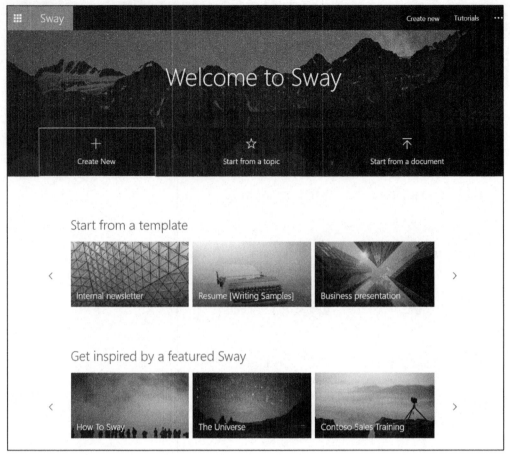

Figure 1.4

Once you start working in Sway, you will see that some additional sections are added in a category called *My Sways* (figure 1.5). Here you can view other projects that you have worked on or viewed etc. At the bottom of the Sway preview, it will show the date it was worked on plus the view count.

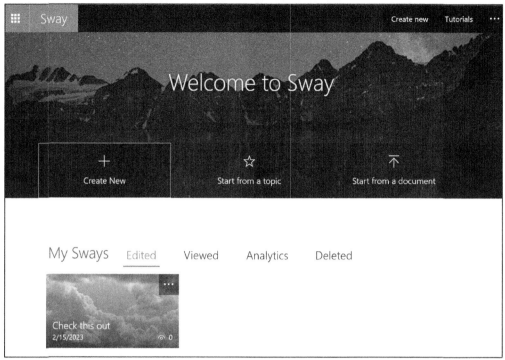

Figure 1.5

If you click on the ellipsis (...) at the upper right of the preview, you will have options to play your Sway, create a link to share your Sway, make a copy of it, or delete the project itself.

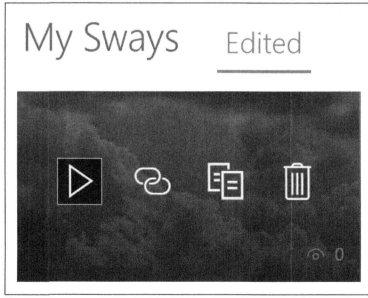

Figure 1.6

When you are in your Sway, you will be able to see all of your cards (discussed later) and also be able to switch between *Storyline* and *Design* view. You can also click on the ellipsis at the upper right to see various options and settings. Also, at the upper right, you will have a *Play* and *Share* button.

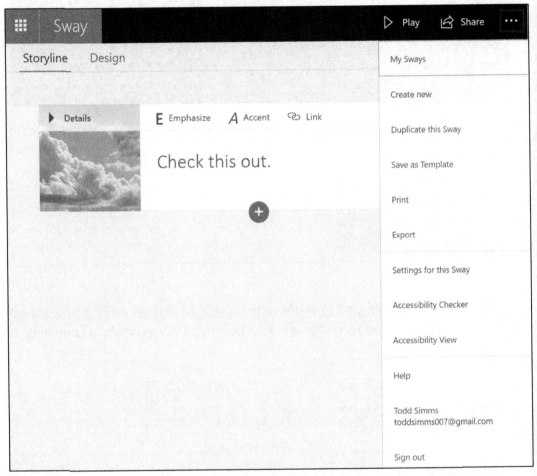

Figure 1.7

Chapter 2 – Adding Content to Your Sway

Now that you have your Microsoft account ready and know how to access the Sway website, it's time to start creating your debut masterpiece. But before you start your work, you will need to decide how you want to begin the process. There are several ways to go about creating your Sway so you might want to try the various options to see which works the best for you.

Starting From a Topic, Document or Blank Sway
When you are on the main Sway page, you will see at the top how you have the choice to create a new Sway which will start from scratch (blank page) as well as starting from a topic or starting from a document. I prefer to start from a blank Sway but I will show you how the other options work so you can decide what works best for you.

Figure 2.1

I will first try the *Start form a topic* option and use Australian Shepherds as the subject of my Sway by typing it in the topic box and clicking on *Create outline*.

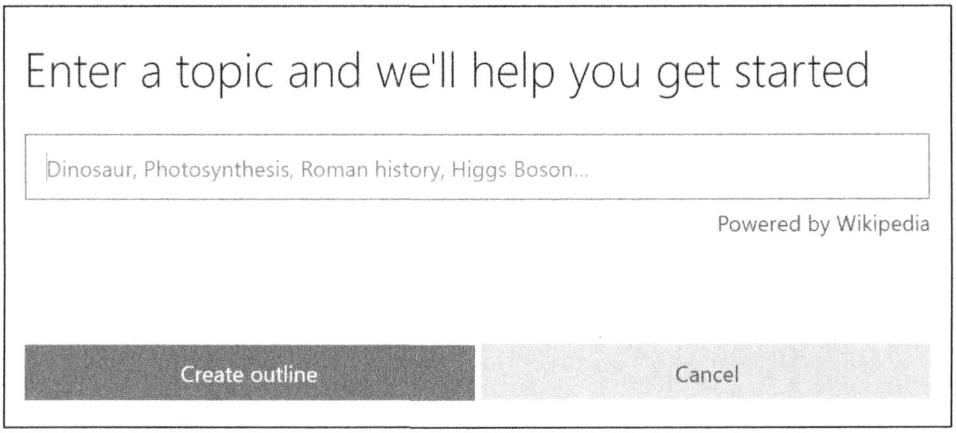

Enter a topic and we'll help you get started

Dinosaur, Photosynthesis, Roman history, Higgs Boson...

Powered by Wikipedia

Create outline   Cancel

Figure 2.2

Sway will then generate some cards based on information it finds for your topic online and add some information or images that go along with them (figures 2.3 through 2.5). At the end of my outline, it will list the references of where it found the information. Then it's up to me to edit the cards, add additional information, or remove anything I don't want.

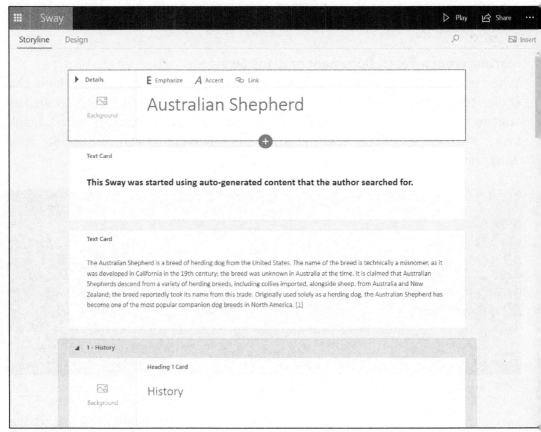

Figure 2.3

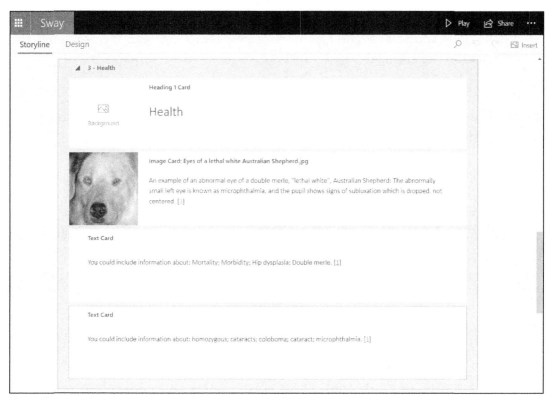

Figure 2.4

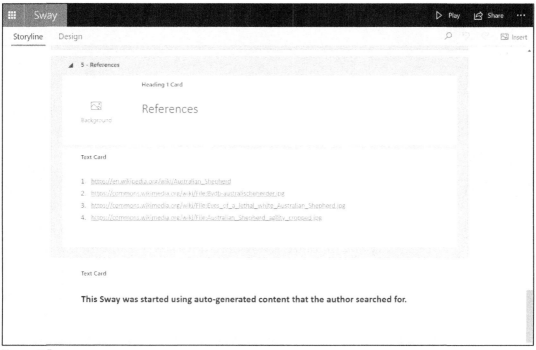

Figure 2.5

As you can see, Sway adds some basic and sort of random information and you might find yourself spending more time removing and rearranging this information than using it.

If I choose the *Start from a document* option, I will need to upload a Word document, PowerPoint presentation or PDF file for Sway to use as its source for the content of my new Sway.

I will upload a PowerPoint file on how to train your puppy which is shown in figure 2.6.

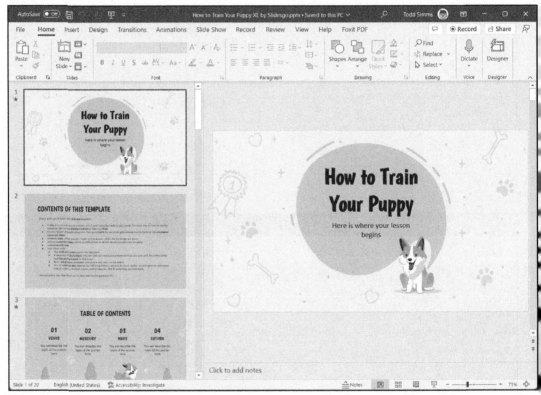

Figure 2.6

As you can see in figure 2.7, Sway will take the information and images from the PowerPoint file and try and organize it to where it makes sense. When you create a Sway using this method, much of the original document formatting is lost but it's a good way to get the basic information from the uploaded file into your Sway.

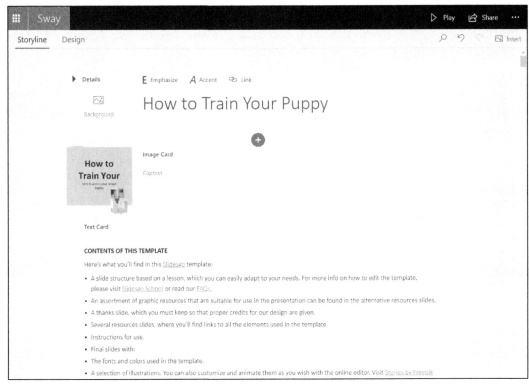

Figure 2.7

Cards

As I mentioned before, I prefer to create my Sways by starting with a blank page. That way I don't need to worry about adjusting any information that was placed by using the start from document or topic methods.

When you create a new Sway using this method, your first card will be created for you. Cards are the building blocks of your Sway and are where you place things such as text, pictures, videos and so on.

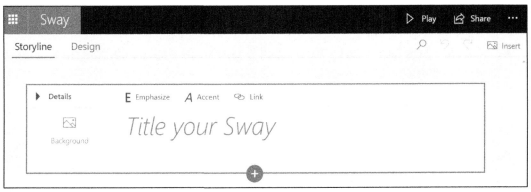

Figure 2.8

The first card is usually used to enter the title for your Sway. Then you can add a background image if you like. You can also use the *Emphasize*, *Accent* and *Link* options to change the look of your card.

To add an additional card, you can simply click on the **+** at the bottom of an existing card to have one added below it. When you add a new card, you will be asked what type of card you wish to add.

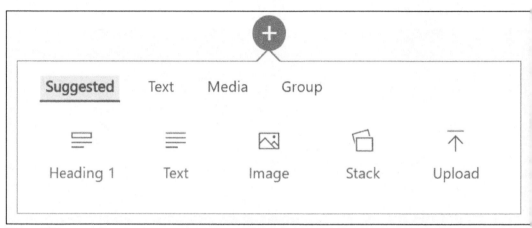

Figure 2.9

Here are what each of these types of cards are used for. I will be going over this information in more detail later in this chapter.

- **Suggested** – Sway will offer suggested card types based on the most commonly used cards.

- **Text** – Here you can add heading text or standard text depending on your needs.

- **Media** – This includes pictures, videos, audio, embedded content and uploaded files.

- **Group** – You can insert various group types for images, comparisons, stacks and slideshows.

For example, if I were to add a text card, it would then be created and placed underneath the card that I created it from as seen in figure 2.10.

Figure 2.10

If I wanted to move this new text card above the card that has my title, I can simply drag and drop it with my mouse to change their order.

When working with cards, you will notice that the menus and icons appear when a particular card is selected. In figure 2.10, the bottom card is selected and in figure 2.11, the top card is selected, and you can see how I now have the options at the top of the title card and the bottom card no longer has the options. You will also notice that the + to add a new card moves to whichever card you have selected.

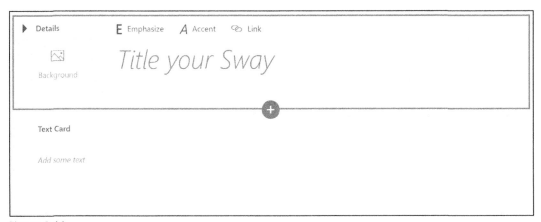

Figure 2.11

Keep in mind that the options you have for a card will vary depending on what type of card you are using. So if you are looking for a particular feature and don't see it on the card, it might be a case that you are not using the right type of card.

It's up to you to decide if you want to create your cards first and then enter the information or complete a card before moving on to the next one. Also, note that it's easy to delete a card by clicking on the trash can icon at the upper right of the card when it's selected.

If you want to copy\duplicate an existing card, all you need to do is check the box at the lower right of the card and use the copy and paste keyboard shortcuts on your computer to make a copy. For Windows, it would be *Ctrl-C* and *Ctrl-V* and for Mac it would be Command-C and Command-V. You will see a message on the card that it has been copied and then you can paste it wherever you like within your Sway.

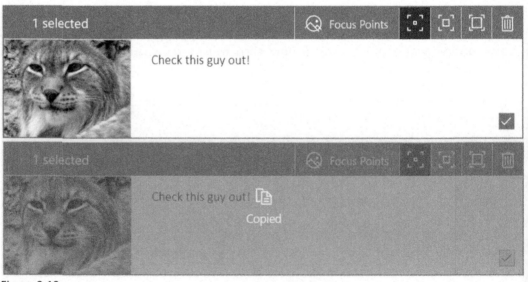

Figure 2.12

 When copying cards from a Sway, you will only be able to paste them into the existing Sway or a different Sway and can't use them in other programs such as Microsoft Word for example. If you try and paste a Sway into Word, it will come out as unusable gibberish.

Adding Text

To add a text to your sway, you will need to first add a text card so you will have the proper text tools to make the text look the way you like. As you can see in figure 2.13, you can add text to other types of cards but if you are looking to add text only, you will most likely want to use a text card.

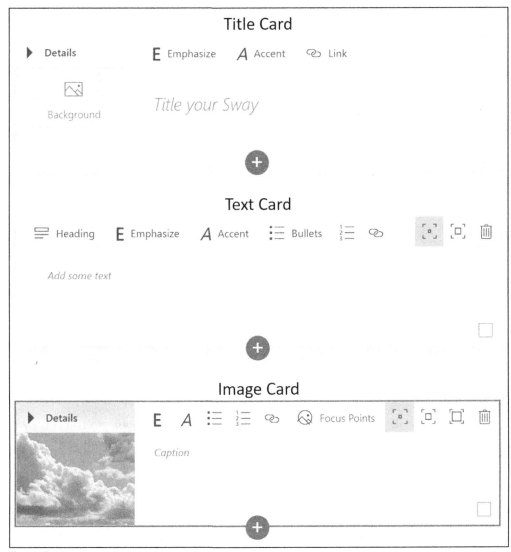

Figure 2.13

Since I have not added any text to my title slide, I will do that first and then add some introductory information to the next text slide. I have decided that my Sway will be about my unfortunately fictional Hawaii vacation. Figure 2.4 shows the results after adding my text. As you can see, it's fairly basic looking but that can be fixed with some formatting which I will be discussing in Chapter 3.

Figure 2.14

You can also copy and paste text from other sources such as documents, emails or websites for example.

Inserting Images

If you want to make your Sway stand out, it's always a good idea to add some photos to help illustrate your point or show examples to go along with your subject matter. When it comes to adding images to your Sway, there are many ways to go about this.

The most common way is to add a new image card and when you do this, you will immediately be given some options as to where you will add your image from as seen in figure 2.15.

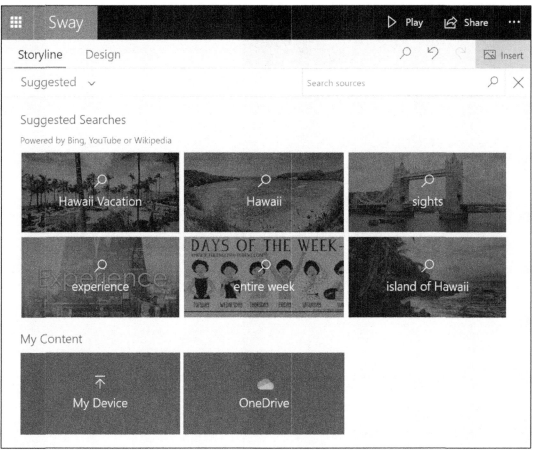

Figure 2.15

As you can see, Sway offers some suggested search options and also give me the option to add pictures that I have on my computer or in my OneDrive online storage account that you get with your Microsoft account. OneDrive is similar to Dropbox and Google Drive which also offer free online storage.

If you would like to learn more about Dropbox or Google Drive, then check out my books titled **Dropbox Made Easy** and **Google Drive Made Easy**.
https://www.amazon.com/dp/B09TN45BSP
https://www.amazon.com/dp/B0BBY4D6FQ

Clicking on the dropdown arrow next to *Suggested* will give you some additional options that you can use to get your images from.

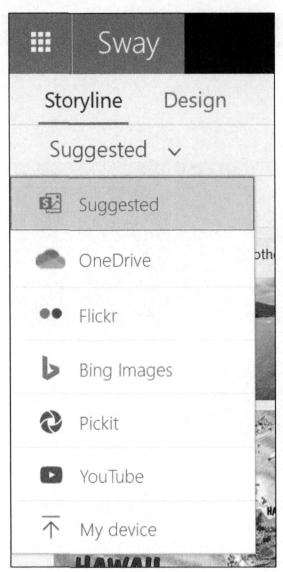

Figure 2.16

If I click on the *Hawaii* suggested search image, I will be shown the results as seen in figure 2.17. These results will also have the image size shown in the lower right corner. The larger the image size, the higher quality the picture will be (most of the time).

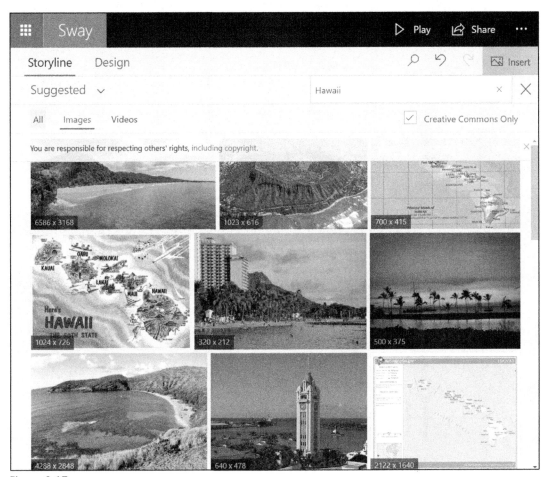

Figure 2.17

If you look at the top right of figure 2.17, you will see a checkbox for *Creative Commons Only*. When this box is checked, Sway will only show you results that are free to use in your project without having to worry about using any copyrighted images. If your Sway is just for personal use then you most likely don't need to worry about only using the free to use images because you will not be using your Sway for websites, publications or advertising where this might be a problem.

I will now choose the first image and click on the *Add* button that will appear after selecting it. Then I will click on the X at the upper right to close the Insert section. Now I will see my image over to the left and I can add some text describing the image if needed.

Figure 2.18

If I click on *Design* at the upper left, I will see how my Sway is coming along to get an idea of how it will look when it's viewed in play mode rather than edit mode. To get back to the editor, simply click on *Storyline*.

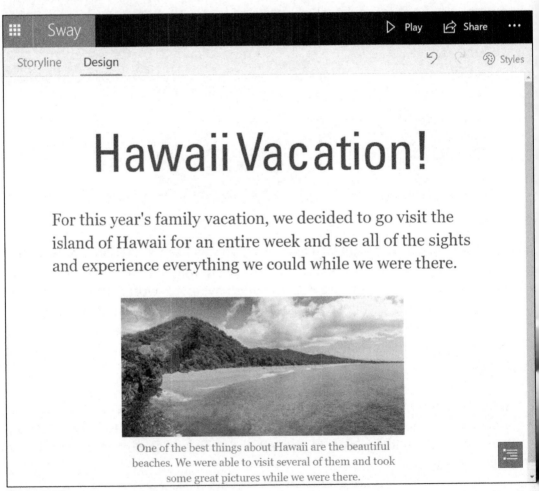

Figure 2.19

Since I am adding images, I will also add a background image to my title slide but this time I will use the *Suggested* dropdown list and choose the *My Device* option to upload a picture from my computer.

If I click on *Details* on my title card, I will then be able to view the text and background image separately and edit them as needed.

Figure 2.20

Image Groups

If you want to add multiple related photos to your Sway and don't want to make a separate image card for each one, you can use an image group card instead. Once you create this card, you will be able to choose between several group types to see what works the best for your photos.

One thing you need to be aware of when making image cards is how you go about adding your images. When you click the new card button and go to the Group section, you will see several types of groups you can create. You can choose the one that you think will work the best for your photos and can then easily change it later after you add your images.

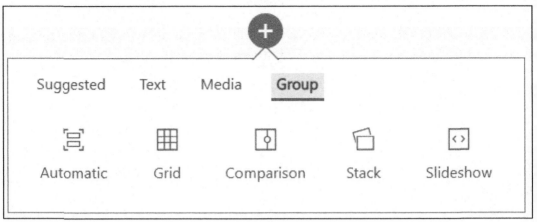

Figure 2.21

I will start with the Grid type of group and figure 2.22 shows how my new card looks.

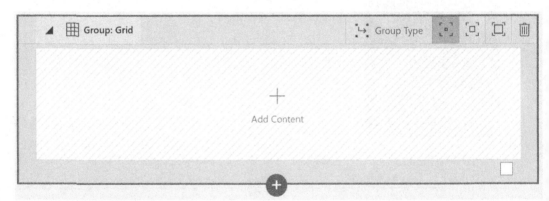

Figure 2.22

As you can see in the upper left, the group type is Grid and there is also a Group Type button at the upper right that you can click on to change the grid type. In the middle, there is a + sign with the words *Add Content* underneath it that you can click on to add your photos.

You will then have four options that you can use to add media to your group. Since I am adding pictures, I can click on *Image* to use the built in pictures or search for some online. Or I can use the *Upload* option to upload them from my computer which is what I will be doing.

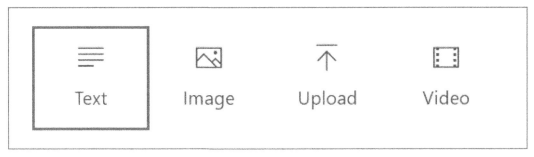

Figure 2.23

One issue you might run into when adding photos this way is that Sway will make separate image cards for each photo even though you used the Add Media option from within the group card (figure 2.24). When this happens, you can drag and drop the image cards into the group card. Figure 2.25 shows the results.

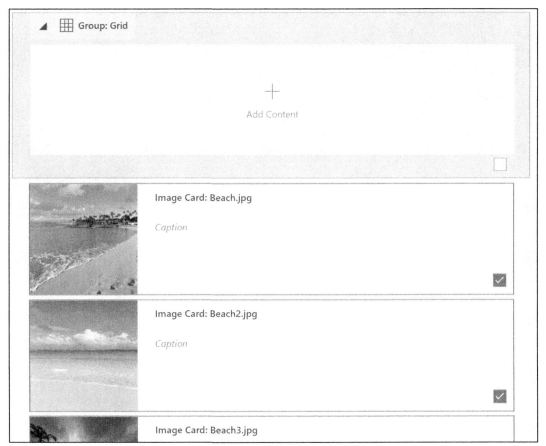

Figure 2.24

You can also see that there is an *Ungroup* option now that all the photos are within the group card.

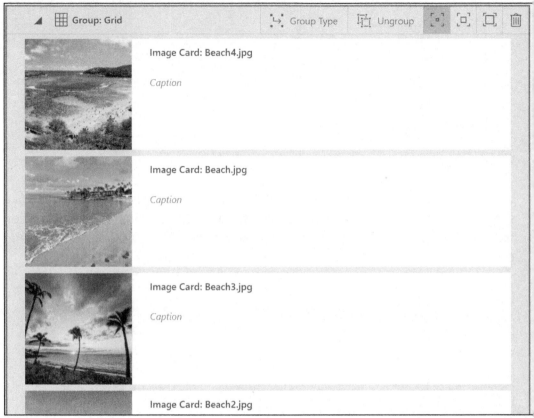

Figure 2.25

Since I only had seven pictures and the grid is in multiples of three, I will have two empty boxes left over in my grid (figure 2.26).

Figure 2.26

Back in edit mode, I can click on Group Type and then change the type to *Stack* (figure 2.27), and I will have the results as seen in figure 2.28.

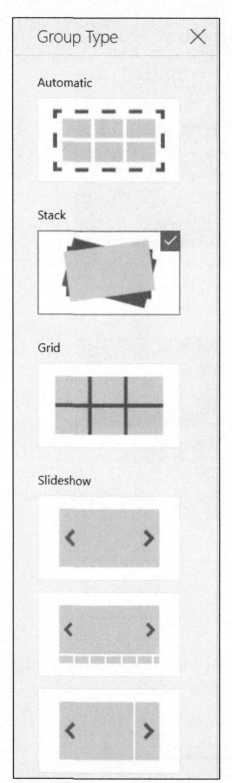

Figure 2.27

Figure 2.28

If I add captions to my photos, they will appear with them as seen in figures 2.29 and 2.30.

Figure 2.29

Figure 2.30

On a side note, if you click the arrow icon at the upper left corner of a card, you can collapse the card content itself so it takes up less room on your screen, so you don't have to scroll up and down as much while working on your Sway.

Figure 2.31

Inserting Videos

If you would like to add a video to your Sway, you can easily do so using a similar method as you did for photos. First, you will begin by adding a new media card and choosing the video option. You will then immediately be taken to the video media page where you can choose one of the suggested videos or search for a video. I will use the dropdown menu at the upper left and choose *YouTube* and Sway will do a search for Hawaii on YouTube itself. I will then select the second video in the results and click on the *Add* button.

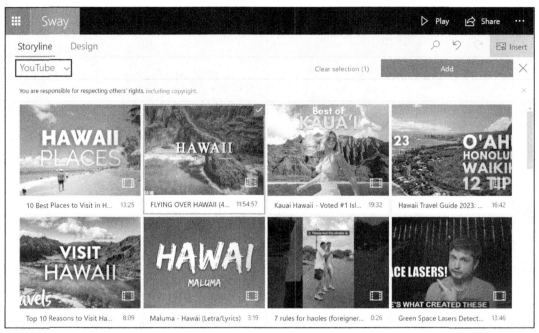

Figure 2.32

As you can see at the bottom of figure 2.33, my video card is under my image group card, and I also added some text to describe the video.

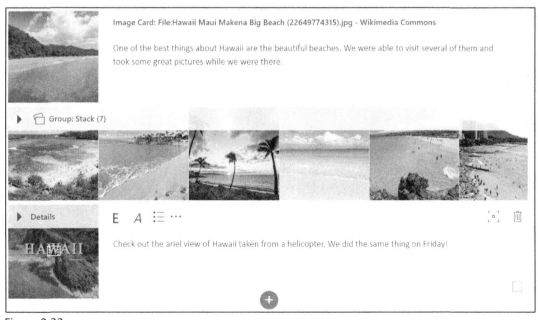

Figure 2.33

If I switch to the Design view, I can get an idea of how my Sway is now coming along with my photo group and new video.

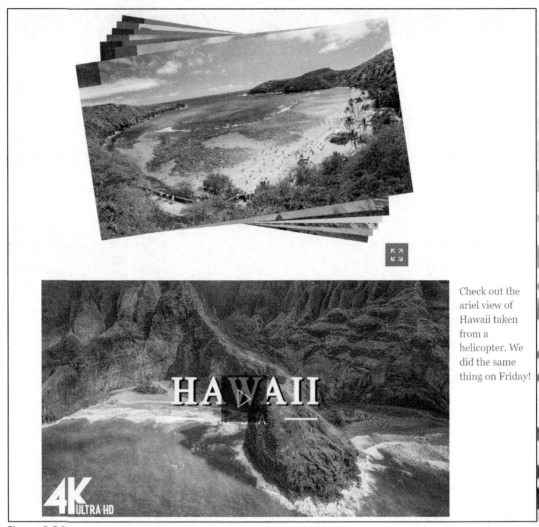

Check out the ariel view of Hawaii taken from a helicopter. We did the same thing on Friday!

Figure 2.34

Inserting Links

Using links is a helpful way to share information with your viewers so you can easily take them to websites, allow them to view online files, or even provide them an email address they can click on to compose a message to a particular person.

You can add a link to an existing card by clicking the create a hyperlink button in the toolbar at the top of the card as seen in figure 2.35.

Figure 2.35

Once you click this button, you will need to type in the text you want to be displayed for your link and then the link itself. You can have the display text and web link text match if you want to just show the link details itself. I will add a link to the helicopter tours website and type in some descriptive text to have displayed in my card. Figure 2.37 shows the results.

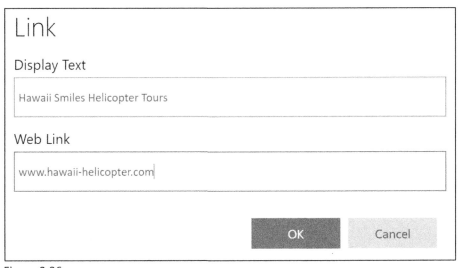

Figure 2.36

Figure 2.37

Now when someone clicks on the *Hawaii Smiles Helicopter Tours* link, it will take them to the associated website within their web browser.

Uploading Content

If you have any files such as Word documents, PDFs, PowerPoint presentations and so on, you can easily add them to your Sway so your viewers will be able to access the information contained within these files. To accomplish this, you will need to choose the *Upload* option when creating a new Media card.

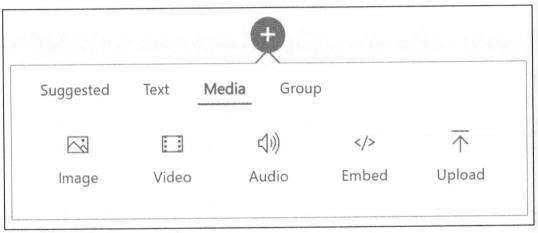

Figure 2.38

I will then choose a Word document about Hawaii tourism that I have located on my computer.

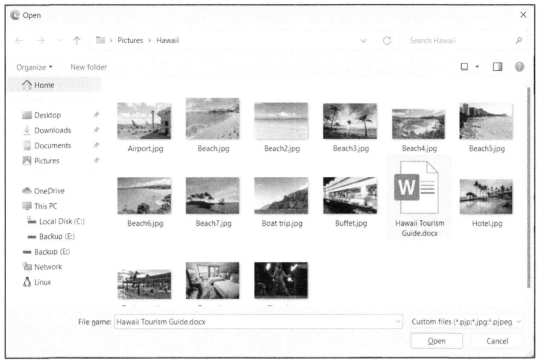

Figure 2.39

When you upload a file, you will have the option to import the contents of the file or embed the file into your Sway so it can be viewed in its original format.

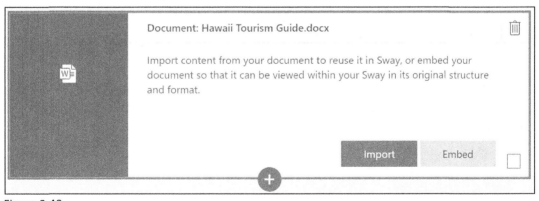

Figure 2.40

If I choose the Import option, my document will be broken down into cards and Sway will do its best to try and organize them so they make sense as shown in figure 2.41. I don't find this method too helpful unless my uploaded document is fairly basic and then I can edit the cards as necessary.

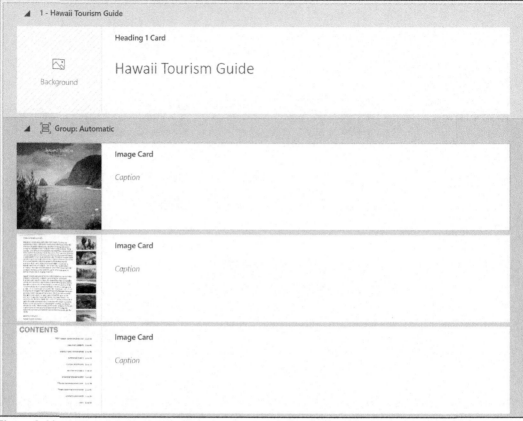

Figure 2.41

If you choose the Embed option, then Sway will add the uploaded file to your project, and you can see the results in figure 2.43 where my video is on the top and my newly embedded Word document is below that.

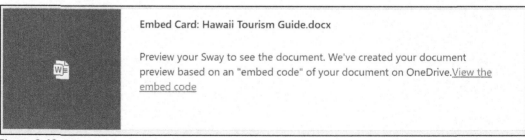

Figure 2.42

Figure 2.43

I can then scroll through the pages right from this screen or click on the full screen button at the lower right to have the document opened in its own window full size.

Chapter 3 – Formatting

When working on your Sways, you might want to focus on getting all of the information in place first before worrying about making it look "pretty". Or you can always do your formatting as you go along. Even if I choose to format as I go, I usually end up changing things at the end to make everything fit together.

In this chapter, I will be discussing how you can format your Sway to make it really stand out and grab your viewer's attention. Keep in mind that you don't get the same number or types of formatting options that you do with let's say Microsoft PowerPoint, but you will have enough options to make things look nice.

Formatting Text
You don't have too many options when it comes to formatting your text. As you can see in figure 3.1, the formatting options for a title card consist of *Emphasize* (bold) and *Accent* (italicize). For text cards, you can also add bullet and number lists. If you click on *Heading*, it will turn your text card into a header card which is good for separating parts of your Sways into different sections.

Figure 3.1

Figure 3.2 shows my title card after applying both of the formatting options. Figure 3.3 shows my text card after adding a bulleted list and using the emphasize option on the line of text above the list. You can also use Styles to add more flair to your Sway and I will be discussing these later in this chapter.

Figure 3.2

Figure 3.3

Card Emphasis

Another way you can make your cards stand out is to set the emphasis level on the card itself. Certain cards will have certain levels that you can use while other cards such as your title card will not offer that option.

Figure 3.4 shows my image card and at the upper right, I have the option to set the emphasis level to subtle, moderate or intense.

Figure 3.4

Figure 3.5 shows how my image card looks when set to subtle while figure 3.6 shows how it looks when set to intense.

Here were our favorite places to go.

- Hanalei Bay

- Waikiki Beach

- Pololu Valley Lookout

- Cafe Pesto

- Manta & Pavilion Wine Bar

One of the best things about Hawaii are the beautiful beaches. We were able to visit several of them and took some great pictures while we were there.

Figure 3.5

Here were our favorite places to go.

- Hanalei Bay
- Waikiki Beach
- Pololu Valley Lookout
- Cafe Pesto
- Manta & Pavilion Wine Bar

One of the best things about Hawaii are the beautiful beaches. We were able to visit several of them and took some great pictures while we were there.

Figure 3.6

When changing the emphasis, always be sure to check the design view so you can see if you are overdoing it or if the level looks correct.

Styles & Remix!

Another way to make your Sways stand out is to apply a style to your project. Sway has many built in styles to choose from and these will do things such as change the color scheme, change the font or apply custom backgrounds to your work.

To get to the style settings, you will need to go into design view and then you will have a *Styles* option at the upper right hand corner. Figure 3.7 shows my Sway before applying any style as well as the style options over to the right.

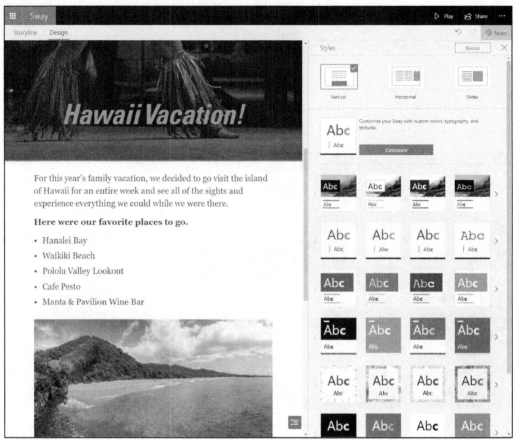

Figure 3.7

Figure 3.8 shows my Sway after applying a style that added a custom background, changed the font and also added some customization to my photos.

 To view additional styles, you can click the left and right arrows to scroll through the options. If you apply a style and don't like it, you can click the undo button above the Remix button to revert the change.

For this year's family vacation, we decided to go visit the island of Hawaii for an entire week and see all of the sights and experience everything we could while we were there.

Here were our favorite places to go.

- Hanalei Bay
- Waikiki Beach
- Pololu Valley Lookout
- Cafe Pesto
- Manta & Pavilion Wine Bar

One of the best things about Hawaii are the beautiful beaches. We were able to visit several of them and took some great pictures while we were there.

Hawaii Tourism Gui...

Figure 3.8

If you click the *Customize* button as seen in figure 3.7, you can do things such as change the color and font settings used with a particular style.

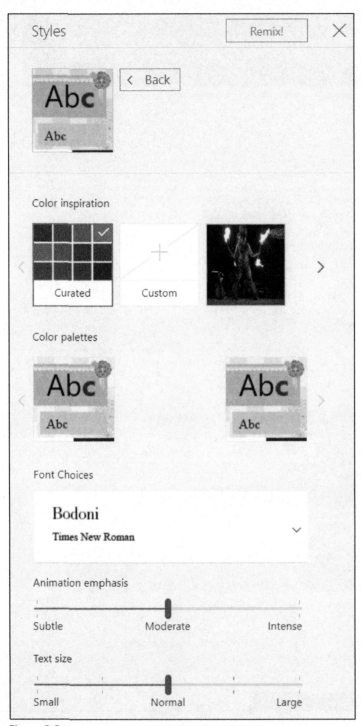

Figure 3.9

If you want to have Sway randomly change the look of your project, then you can click on the *Remix!* button. This will apply a random style every time you click on the button, and you can keep clicking until you find a look that you like.

48

Focus Points

Depending on the layout you use for your image cards and the size of your pictures, you might find that certain parts of them get cut off and they might not look the way you intended them to look. Fortunately, there is an easy way to tell Sway exactly which part of your photo to display in your work.

While in a card with an image, you can click on the *Focus Points* button and then you can then tell Sway what part of your image to show in your presentation. Figure 3.10 shows my title card with the full image and below that I am shown a preview of how the image will be displayed on a computer as well as on a smartphone. As you can see, the top part of the image has been cut off.

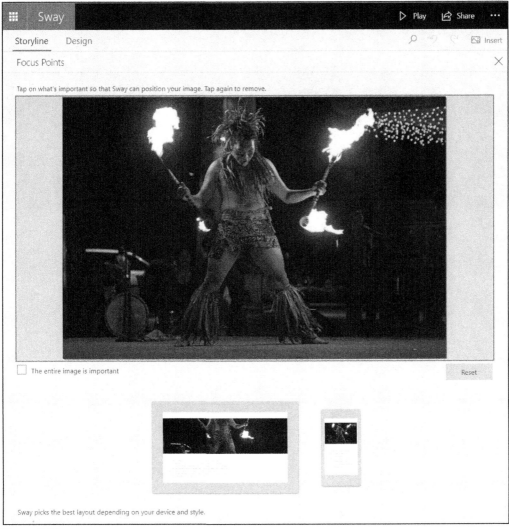

Figure 3.10

If I click on a spot on the image, Sway will add a circle indicating the focus point for that picture. Figure 3.11 shows the results after adding a focus point to the face of the performer.

Figure 3.11

You can also use multiple focus points to create an area on your photo that you want to be displayed. To remove a focus point, simply click on it again.

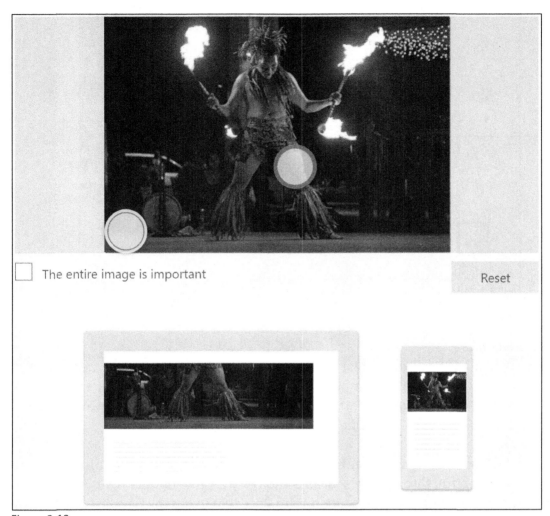

Figure 3.12

If you want the entire image to be shown in your Sway, you can check the box that says *The entire image is important*. Just keep in mind that it might appear on the smaller side in order to fit the entire picture on the screen.

Figure 3.13

Templates

If you don't feel like starting from scratch for your new Sway, you can check out some of the included templates to see if you can find one that matches the concept of your Sway. Unfortunately, you can't apply a theme to an existing Sway and will have to choose your theme before you get started.

From the main Sway page, find the section that says *Start from a template* and you can scroll through the available choices with the left and right arrows. I will choose the theme titled *Vacation story* since it matches my Hawaii vacation idea.

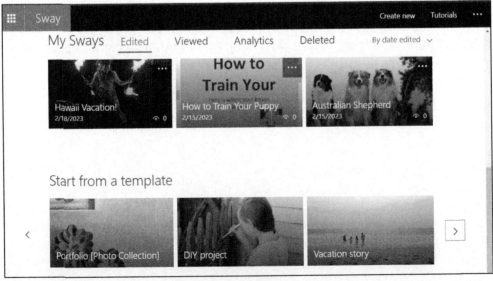

Figure 3.14

Once you load the theme and click on start editing, you will see its layout in your storyline. As you can see in figure 3.15, Sway created a title slide, image card, text card and some others that are not shown. I can then edit these cards with the information about my Hawaii vacation and remove any cards that I don't need.

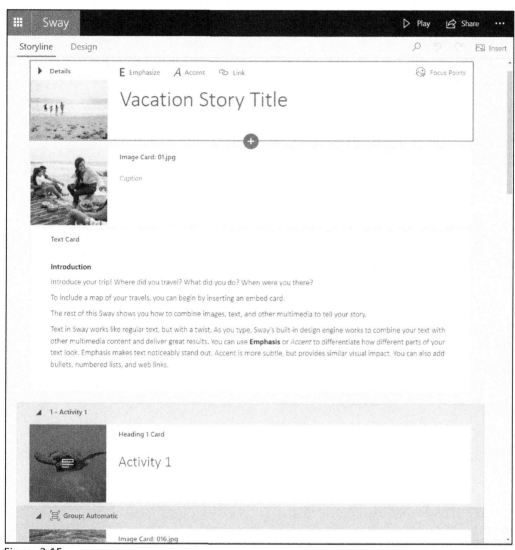

Figure 3.15

If you have spent a lot of time customizing your Sway and think you might want to use its layout for future projects, you can easily save your current Sway as a template so you can apply it to a new Sway.

To do so, click on the ellipsis (...) at the upper right hand corner and choose *Save as Template*.

Play
Share
My Sways
Create new
Duplicate this Sway
Save as Template

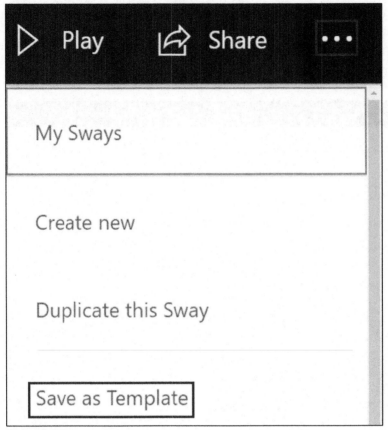

Figure 3.16

You will then need to choose a template name. It will use the title card name by default if you don't change it.

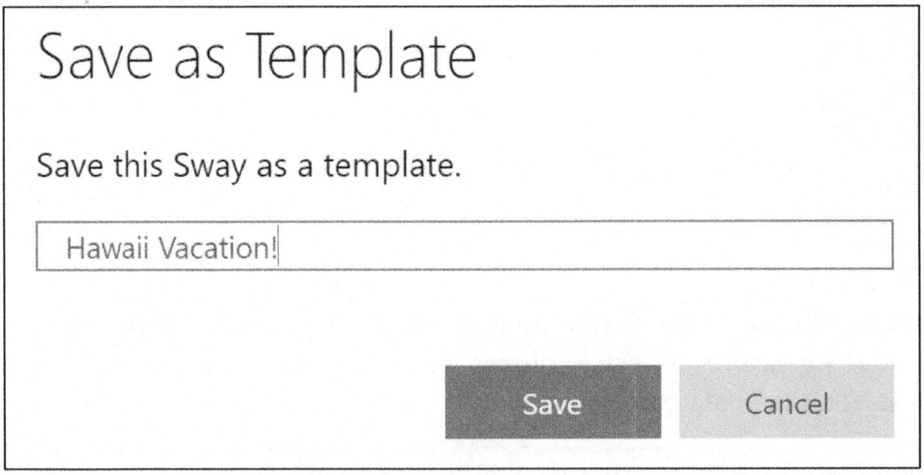

Save as Template
Save this Sway as a template.
Hawaii Vacation!
Save
Cancel

Figure 3.17

Now when you go back to the main page and look in the template section, you will see your newly created template.

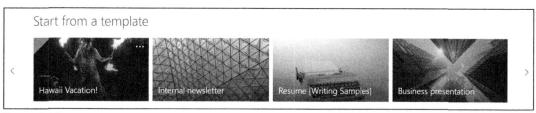

Figure 3.18

Featured Sways

You might have noticed the section at the bottom of the main Sway screen called Featured Sways. This is there simply to give you ideas of how you can organize and format the information for your own Sways. As of now, you cannot use any of these Sways as a template but can only view them.

If I were to click on the Sway titled *Contoso Sales Training*, I would be able to play it as well as view its outline layout as seen in figure 3.20.

Figure 3.19

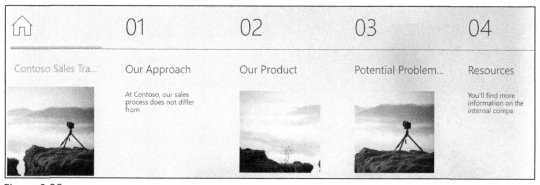

Figure 3.20

Storyline, Design and Section Views

Even though I have been using both the storyline and design views so far throughout this book, I just wanted to mention them so you know the difference between the two. I also wanted to take a moment to discuss the section view since you might find that it comes in handy as well.

The storyline view is where you will be doing all of your editing such as adding new cards, text, images, videos and so on and is what you have seen the most of so far in this book.

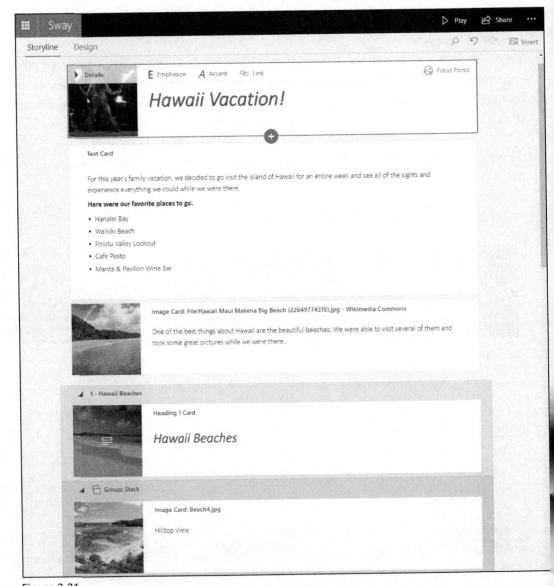

Figure 3.21

The design view is what you use to see how your work will look when others view it. It's similar to playing your Sway but it's a faster way to navigate between your working view (storyline) and a preview of how your final design will look (figure 3.22).

Figure 3.22

When you are in design view, you can click the button at the lower right corner as seen in figure 3.22 to see the section view. If you have multiple heading cards, they will be used to break your Sway into sections or groups. I added a couple of heading cards to my Sway so you can see how it works as shown in figure 3.23. You can then click on any of the sections to be taken to that part of your Sway.

Figure 3.23

Card Views, Auto Play & Animations

During the Sway creation process, you might want to consider playing your Sway to see how it is coming along. Sure, you can use the design view, but the Play feature will really show you how the finished result will look. The Play button can be found at the upper right of the Sway interface.

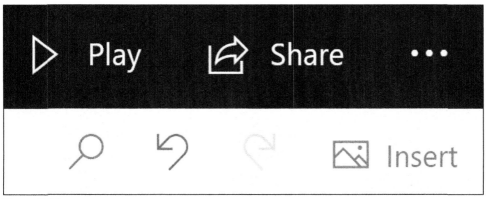

Figure 3.24

When you play your Sway, you have three different ways you can view it as seen in the *Change layout* section in figure 3.25. You can access these settings by clicking on the gear icon while playing your Sway. The default view is to scroll your sway vertically, but you can also choose horizontally or play it as a slide show which works in a similar manner to PowerPoint.

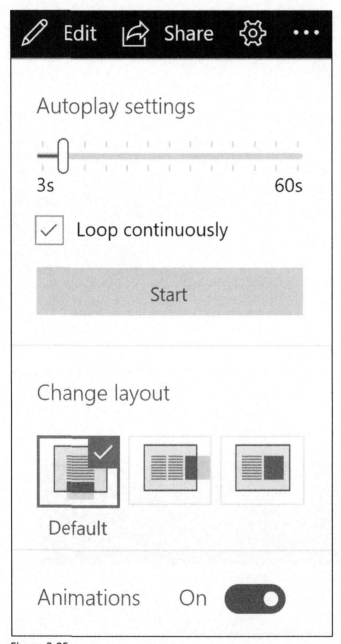

Figure 3.25

If you choose the default or horizontal layouts, you can scroll through your Sway using the wheel on your mouse or the arrow keys on your keyboard. If you use the horizontal or slide layout, you will have a left and right button at the bottom of the screen next to the section view button. The button to the left of the arrow buttons is used to view your sections which is sort of like a table of contents.

Figure 3.26

The *Autoplay* setting is used to play your Sway automatically, so you do not need to click or scroll through each slide or card. Just because the box it checked for Autoplay doesn't mean it will start on its own. You will need to come to this setting and then click on the *Start* button. The time slider is used to set how many seconds each card is shown on the screen before it moves to the next one. The *Loop continuously* checkbox is used to repeat your Sway when it gets to the end.

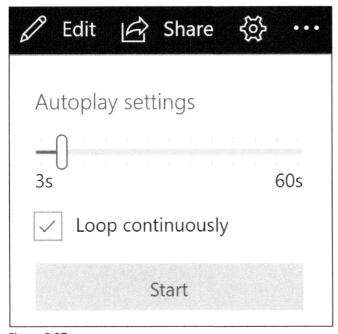

Figure 3.27

The *Animations* on or off slider is used to enable or disable animations for text and images and will do things such as make the text slide across the screen into position and make photos appear or stretch out into place.

 To exit the play mode while manually scrolling through your cards or even when playing your Sway automatically, simply click anywhere on the page and then click the X that appears at the upper right-hand corner.

Accessibility Checker

One thing to keep in mind when designing your Sways is that just because everything looks good to you and is easy to read, doesn't mean it will be that way for everyone. Sway has an accessibility checker that you can run from the ellipsis at the upper right-hand corner.

This will show you an overall listing of things you might want to check such as alternative text for images that can be read with special software that might be used by those with vision impairments. This alt text can be used to describe an image in case it can't be seen clearly by your viewer.

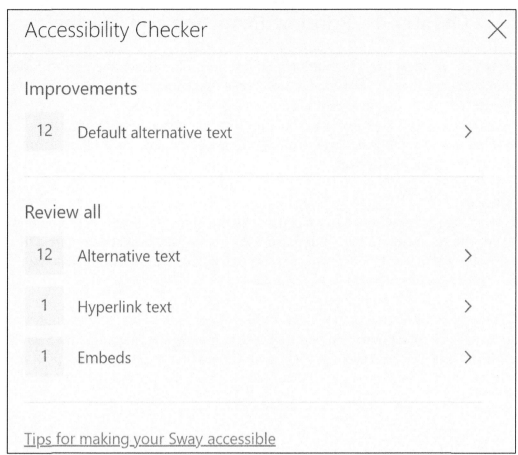

Figure 3.28

When you click on one of the sections to review, Sway will give you a suggestion as to what it thinks you should do to ensure that your Sway is viewable by everyone.

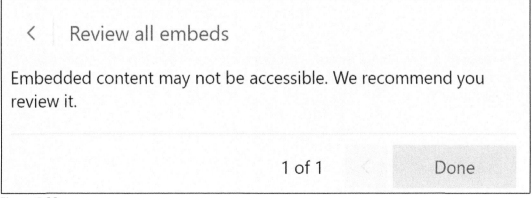

Figure 3.29

Chapter 4 – Printing, Exporting and Sharing

Since you will most likely be putting a bit of effort into making the perfect Sway, it makes sense that you will want other people to be able to see it and enjoy it for themselves. Or if you have created your Sway as a type of business advertisement or promotion, you might want to share it on social media. Fortunately, there are several ways to get your Sway from your computer and onto other people's computers or mobile devices.

Printing

Even though printing your Sway might not be the most practical or common thing to do, you still have the option to do so. Let's say you used Sway to create a flyer or poster which would most likely only be one page. This is a perfect example of the type of Sway you might want to print.

To print your Sway, click on the ellipsis at the upper right corner of the screen and choose the Print option. You will then see a message telling you that Sway is creating a PDF version of your project. It will do this first to convert it to a printable format. You will then be shown a dialog box with a link to download the PDF file.

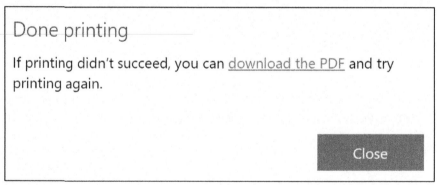

Figure 4.1

Once you click the *Close* button, you can then either print to PDF or print to your actual printer by changing the printer selection from the drop-down list as seen in figure 4.2.

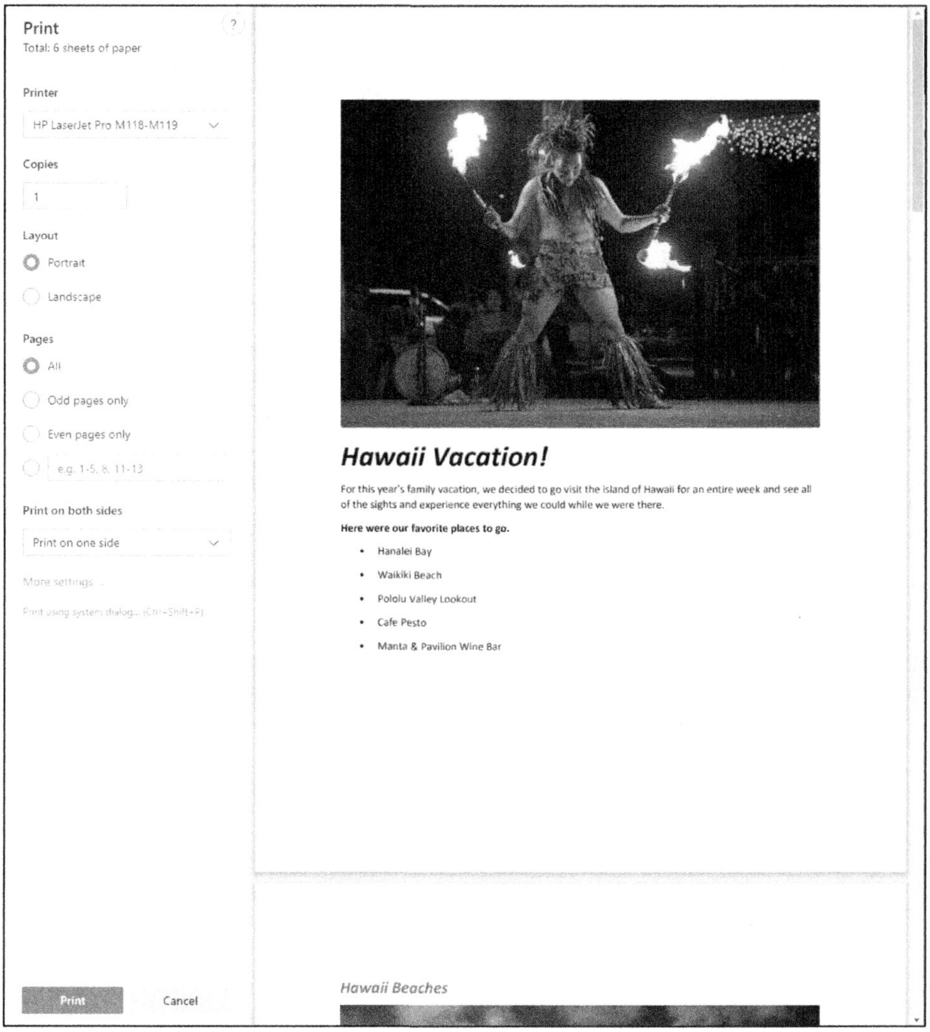

Figure 4.2

Just like with any other print job, you can decide what pages you want to be printed, print on two sides if your printer supports it and also open the settings for your printer to change any printing options that might be necessary.

Exporting

Exporting is similar to printing except you won't be placing your Sway on paper but rather converting it to a file that you can then keep on your computer to edit using a different program. Or you can do things such as email it to other people so they can view or work on it.

You can start the export process from the same area where you find the print selection. When exporting your Sway, you have two options to choose from. You can save it as a Microsoft Word document or as a PDF file.

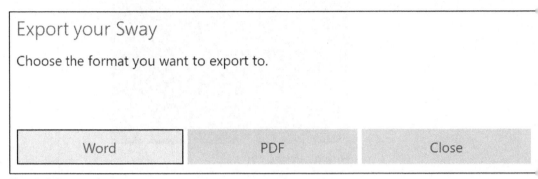

Figure 4.3

If you want to edit your Sway after exporting it then you will most likely want to choose the Word option (assuming you have Word on your computer). PDF files are usually harder to edit and require special editing software.

Whichever option you choose, Sway will download the file to your computer, and you should get a popup notification in your web browser asking you where you want to save your exported file.

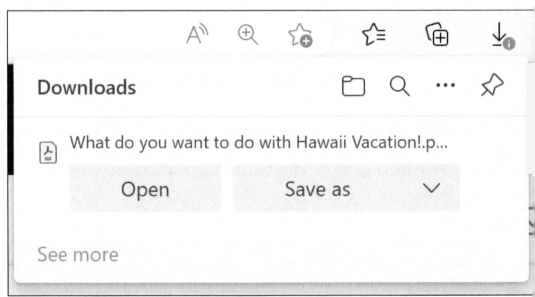

Figure 4.4

PDF files will generally be smaller in size than Word files and might be a better option if you are just planning on giving someone a read only copy of your Sway and don't want them making any changes to it. Figure 4.5 shows my exported Sway as a Word document and also as a PDF file. As you can see, the Word version is 3.23 MB (megabytes) while the PDF version is less than 1 MB.

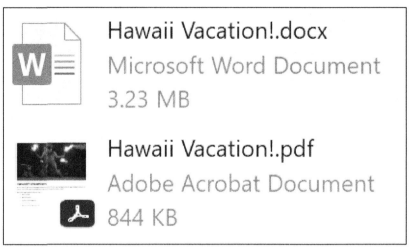

Figure 4.5

When it comes to sending documents\files via email, you need to be aware that there are limits on how large of a file you can send as an attachment. If you send one that is too large, it will be rejected at the other end so try and keep attachments under 10-15 MB.

When viewing either a Word or PDF copy of your Sway, they should look very similar. Figure 4.6 shows a Word version while figure 4.7 shows a PDF version.

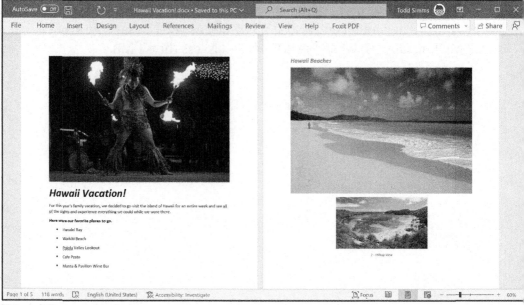

Figure 4.6

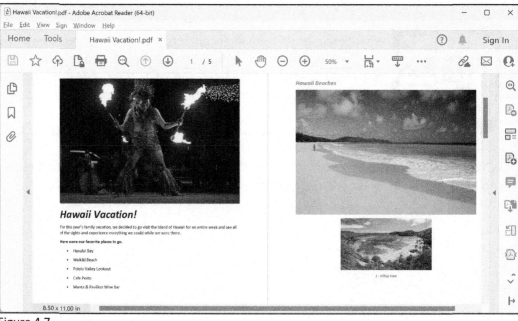

Figure 4.7

Sharing

With the increased popularity of online apps such as Gmail, Google Docs, Office 365, Slack and so on, comes the ease with which we can share our work with coworkers or even friends and family. Rather than have to email files back and forth, we can simply share our work right from the app and send an invitation or link for others to use to open our documents, projects, files etc. on their end.

Sway offers many ways to share your work with others so you should be able to find a method that does the job for you. Or maybe you will find all of the sharing methods useful!

To share your Sway, you can click on the *Share* button at the top right of the page and you will be shown all of the sharing options as seen in figure 4.8. If you click on *More options*, you will see that you can assign a password to your shared Sway, have other viewers see the Share button so they can then share it and reset the sharing settings to their default.

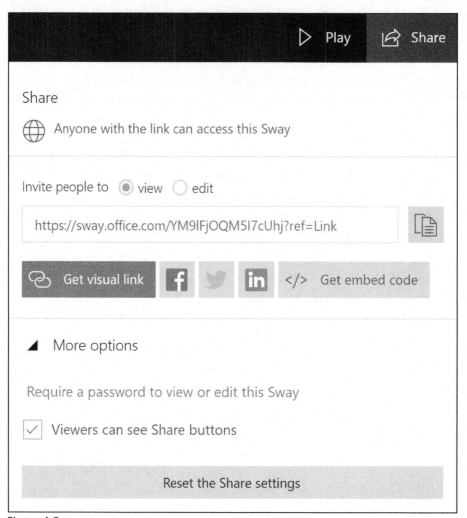

Figure 4.8

The most common way to share a Sway is to copy the link provided in the box at the top of the screen. You can give others the ability to only view your Sway or to edit our Sway if you want them to be able to make changes.

The button that says *Get visual link* is similar to creating a shared link except it will show the beginning part of your Sway as a type of preview with an image rather than just a basic text link (figure 4.9).

Keep in mind that not all email clients will support pasting in this type of link so if it only pastes the text, then you will know that its most likely an issue with your email app rather than you are doing something incorrectly.

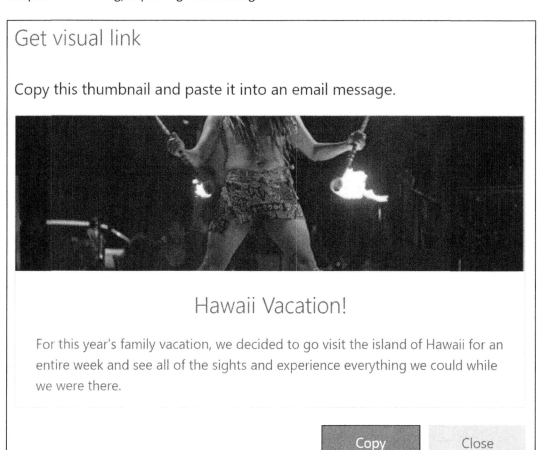

Get visual link

Copy this thumbnail and paste it into an email message.

Hawaii Vacation!

For this year's family vacation, we decided to go visit the island of Hawaii for an entire week and see all of the sights and experience everything we could while we were there.

Copy   Close

Figure 4.9

The *Embed* option can be used to create an embed link that can then be used to show your Sway on a web page or other platform that supports embedded links.

Embed this Sway

<iframe width="760px" height="500px" src="https://sway.office.com/s/YM9IFjOQN

Copy to Clipboard   Close

Figure 4.10

Finally, you can share your Sway on various social media platforms such as Facebook, Twitter and LinkedIn. Once you click on the associated icon in the sharing section, you will be taken to that social media site where you will need to log in and then you can post your sway just like you would any other content. Figure 4.11 shows how my Sway looks when it's shared on Facebook.

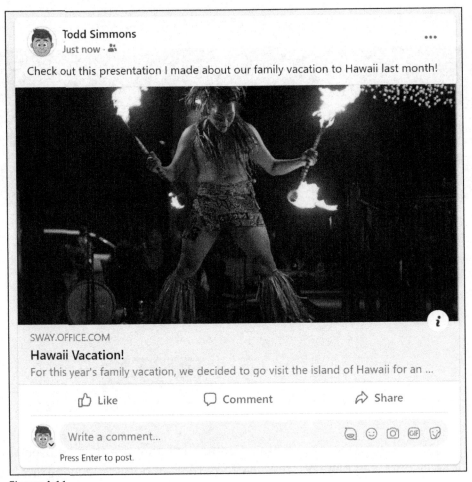

Figure 4.11

Chapter 5 – Extras

In this chapter, I want to discuss some of the other Sway features that don't necessarily fit in the other chapters but are still important to know about. Overall, Sway is a fairly basic app but there are some things that are worth discussing that might not be super obvious.

Settings

Most apps and programs have settings that you can adjust that affect how the app itself works. But for Sway, the settings apply to the particular Sway you are working on itself. This is a nice feature because you can apply different settings to different Sways as needed.

To access the settings, while in the Sway you want the settings to apply to, go to the ellipsis and then choose *Settings for this Sway*. You will then see all of the settings you can apply to that particular Sway as seen in figure 5.1.

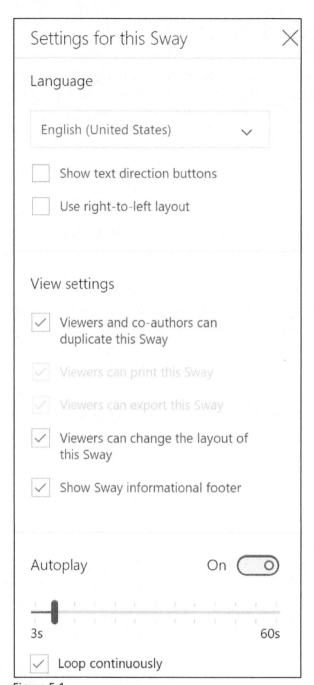

Figure 5.1

Here is what each of these settings will do.

- **Show text direction buttons** – This will give you extra buttons in your card that will allow you to change the direction of the text within that card.

Figure 5.2

- **Use right-to-left layout** – This will allow you to change the way the text is displayed from the default left to right to right to left.

- **Viewers and co-authors can duplicate this Sway** – If you have this box checked, people you have shared your Sway with will be able to copy your Sway when opening it on their computer.

Figure 5.3

- **Viewers can print this Sway** – This will enable printing of your Sway by others who are able to open it.

- **Viewers can export this Sway** – This allows others to export your Sway to a PDF or Word document.

- **Viewers can change the layout of this Sway** – When this is checked, others can change the way your Sway is displayed such as horizontally, vertically, or in a slideshow view.

- **Show Sway informational footer** – You might have noticed that when playing your Sway, when you get to the end there is a message that says *Made with Microsoft Sway*. If you do not want this shown, then simply uncheck this box.

> Made with Microsoft Sway
>
> Create and share interactive reports, presentations,
> personal stories, and more.

Figure 5.4

- **Enable or disable Autoplay** – If you want your Sway to run by itself without you needing to click or scroll through it when playing it, then you can enable this feature here. You can also change how fast your Sway will play when using this method. If you have this checked and play your Sway, you might notice that you are unable to change the view that is used.

Searching

If you end up creating a rather large or in depth Sway, you might find that you have the need to go back and maybe do some editing or find a particular topic you have written about. If so, you can use the built in search feature to find words or phrases within your Sway.

To use the search feature, simply click on the magnifying glass under the Play button and then type in your search in the box that appears below.

Figure 5.5

If I were to search for the word *beach*, I am shown that there are three instances of the word within my Sway, and they are highlighted in yellow making it easier to find them within my project.

Figure 5.6

While in the search mode, you can click on the gear icon next to the search box to enable options for finding whole words only and matching the sentence case for your searches.

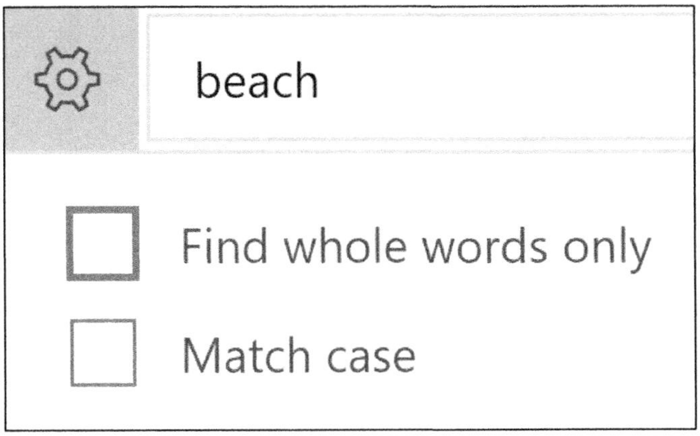

Figure 5.7

Logos

If you are going to be using Sway for something like your business and have a logo for your business, you might want to add it to your Sway to give it more of an "official" look.

To add your logo, go to the storyline and click on the word *Details* at the upper left of your title card.

Figure 58

Then at the bottom of the card, click on *Add a logo*.

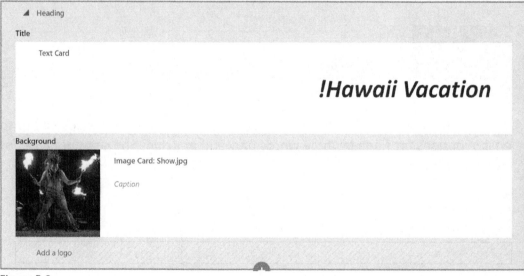

Figure 5.9

You will then need to browse your computer and find your logo file and then select it. It will then be shown at the bottom of the card in the Logo section.

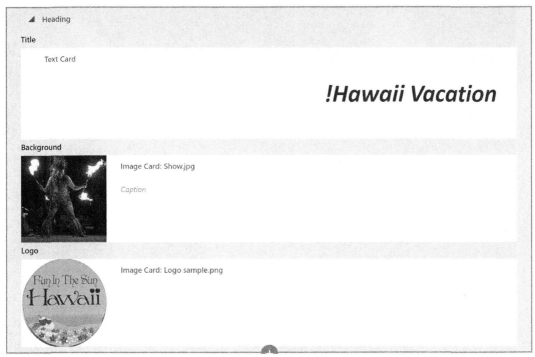

Figure 5.10

When you switch to the design view or play your Sway, you will now see your logo on your title card.

Figure 5.11

When adding a logo to Sway, try and make sure it has a transparent background, so you don't get a white box around your logo assuming it's not a box to begin with. Using transparent PNG files is a good choice when creating logos.

Analytics

Sway has a basic analytics feature that you can use to see how many times your work has been viewed by those you have shared it with and also how much time was spent viewing your Sway.

If you go back to the main Sway page, you will see a section called *Analytics*. This will give you an idea of how much attention your Sway is getting. And when I say idea, I mean that is not super accurate and should be used only to get an overview of how others are viewing your Sway.

My Sways	Edited	Viewed	Analytics	Deleted		
2/22/2023 Hawaii Vacation!	02 Total views	4 min Avg time spent	100% Avg completion	00 glanced 02 quick read 00 deep read		

Figure 5.12

Another way to see how other people are interacting with your Sway is to go back to the sharing settings and at the bottom you will see a section called *Authors* if there is anyone currently working on your Sway.

Figure 5.13

If you hover your mouse over the initials of a person under Authors, you will see their name, email address and if they are viewing or editing your Sway.

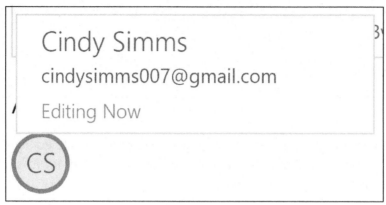

Figure 5.14

From the main Sway page, you can also see how many people have your Sway open from the title card preview image by looking at the lower right hand corner for a number.

Figure 5.15

Clicking on the silhouette icon at the upper right will show you who you have designated as authors for your Sway and have the right to edit your work (figure 5.16).

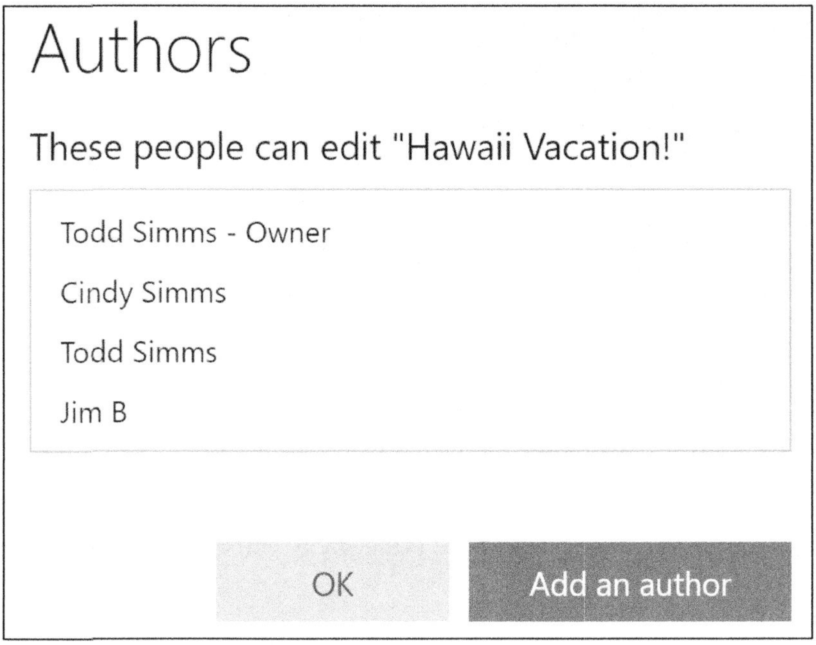

Authors

These people can edit "Hawaii Vacation!"

Todd Simms - Owner

Cindy Simms

Todd Simms

Jim B

OK   Add an author

Figure 5.16

Copying, Deleting and Restoring Sways

Just because you are creating and working on your Sways via the Sway website, doesn't mean you are stuck keeping your work forever. Even though Sways are not actual files like a Word document etc., you can still treat them as so to a certain extent.

If you spent some time creating the perfect Sway and want to duplicate it so you can then make changes while keeping the original intact, you can make a copy of your Sway and then work on the copy.

To make a copy of a Sway, go to the main Sway page where you will see the list of projects you are working on. Then select the Sway you want to copy and click on the ellipsis at the upper right and then click the copy icon as seen in figure 5.17.

Figure 5.17

Next, you will be given the opportunity to rename your Sway or have the copy use the same name as the original. I would rename the copy to make it easier to keep track of.

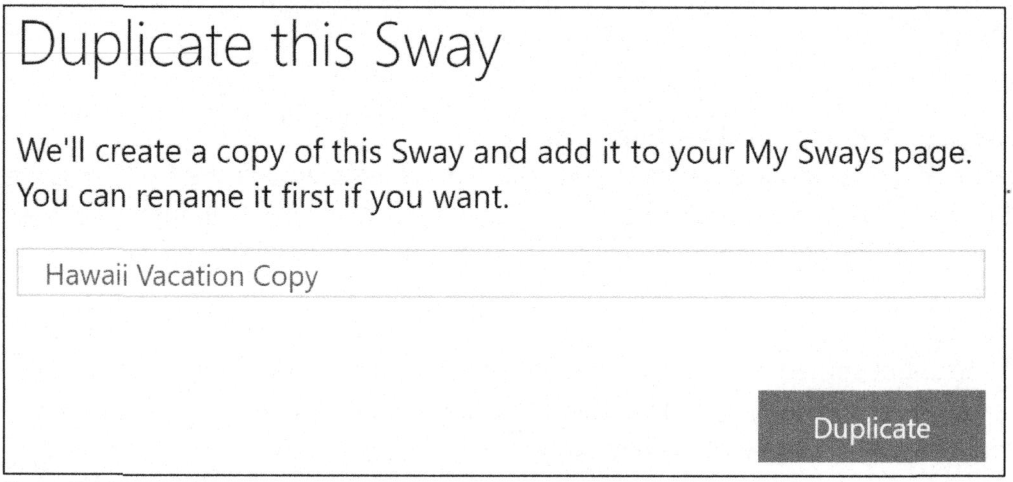

Duplicate this Sway

We'll create a copy of this Sway and add it to your My Sways page. You can rename it first if you want.

Hawaii Vacation Copy

Duplicate

Figure 5.18

Figure 5.19 shows my main Sway list with my original as well as my copy next to it. I can then work on each Sway independently of the other.

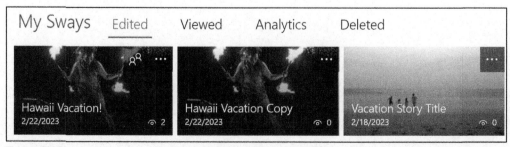

Figure 5.19

If you have any Sways that you decided you do not need any longer, you can easily delete them from this same area. To do so, simply click on the ellipsis on the Sway you want to delete and then click on the trash can icon.

Figure 5.20

 Another task you can accomplish after clicking on the ellipsis for a Sway in your main Sway listing is to create a link to share your Sway. To do so, click on the link icon next to the play button and then you will be shown a sharing link that you can then copy on the spot.

Once you have deleted a Sway, it will be placed in the "trash" similar to how files are placed in the recycle bin when you delete them on your computer (for Windows that is). To view your deleted items, you can go to the Deleted section as seen in figure 5.21.

Figure 5.21

From here you can restore a Sway that has previously been deleted as well as permanently delete one or more Sways from the trash. Once a Sway has been deleted, it will be removed from the trash for good after 30 days and you will not have any way of getting it back.

Sway Desktop App

For those of you who prefer working from an app rather than a website, Sway has its own desktop app that you can download for free and use with your account. You can think of it as being similar to using Word online from the Microsoft Office website compared to using the Word desktop software installed on your computer.

To download and install the app, go to the Microsoft Store on your computer (Windows only) and do a search for Sway. Once you find it, click on the *Get* button to have it installed on your computer. Just make sure you are installing the correct app. It should have a green logo with a white S in the middle and the author should be Microsoft Corporation.

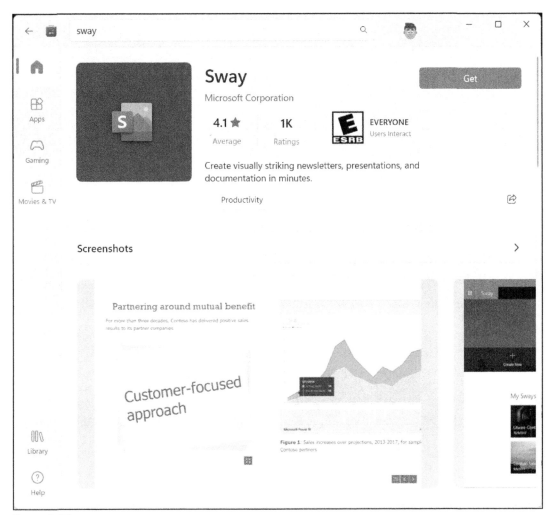

Figure 5.22

Once you open the Sway app, you will see that the main Sway page and your Sways themselves look and function exactly the same way as they do on the Sway website (figures 5.23 & 5.24). You will need to be logged into the app to use it and will be prompted to do so if necessary.

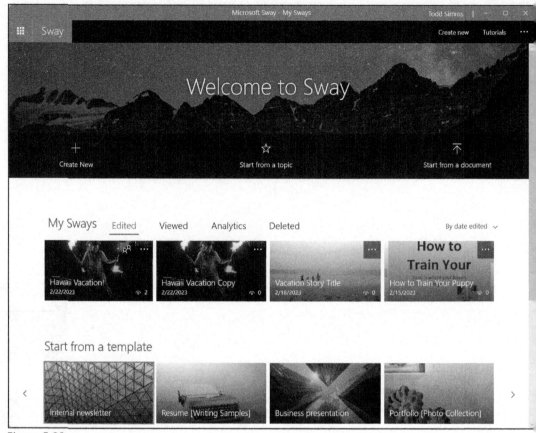

Figure 5.23

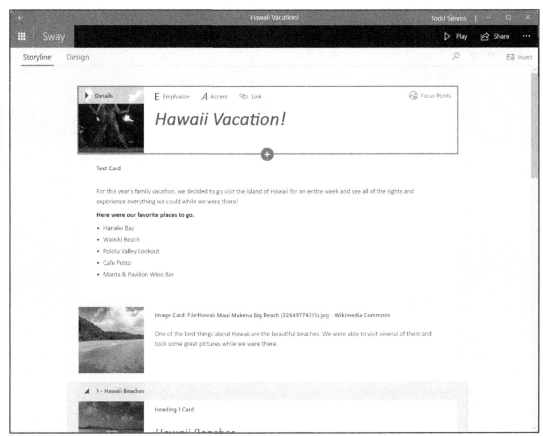

Figure 5.24

Getting Help

Even though Sway is fairly basic and there is not too much to it, you might still find yourself getting stuck trying to figure out how to do something or wondering why a certain feature doesn't work.

Sway itself does not have a built-in help feature like many programs do but rather relies on resources you can find online to get the answers you are looking for. So when you click on the ellipsis at the upper right and choose *Help*, you have a couple of options to choose from as seen in figure 5.25.

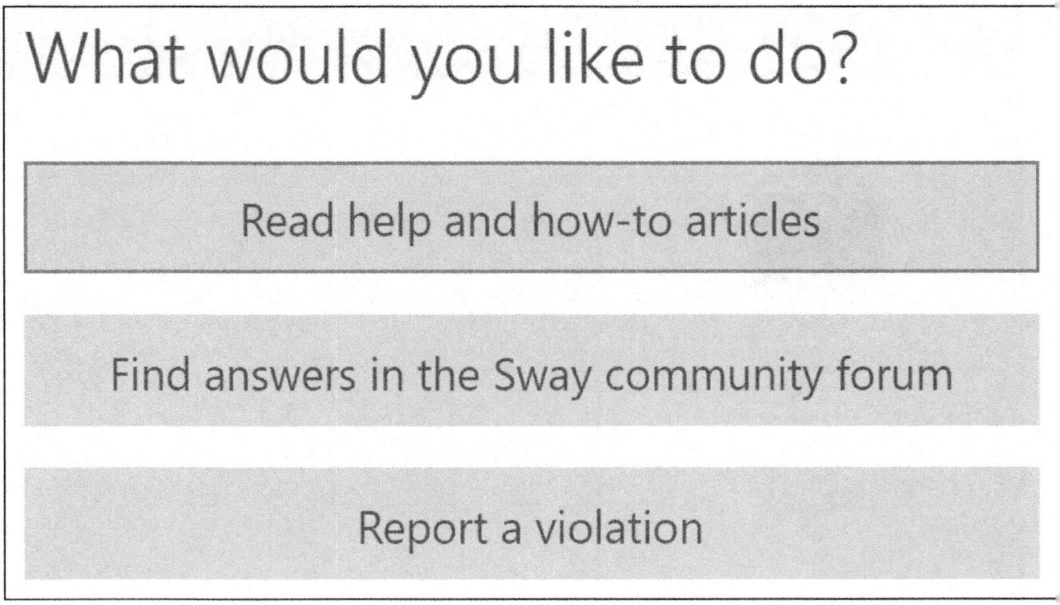

What would you like to do?

Read help and how-to articles

Find answers in the Sway community forum

Report a violation

Figure 5.26

The *Read help and how-to articles* button will take you to the Sway website where you can check out the latest articles and videos on how to use Sway. This content will most likely change from time to time as it gets updated.

The *Find answers in the Sway community forum* button will take you to the Microsoft online forum where you can log in and then post your question so other Sway users can suggest answers for you. You can also post answers to other users' questions if you feel like helping someone else out.

One thing you might notice about the forum is that there is no Sway specific section, and you will need to select *Other* from the apps dropdown list before asking your question.

What's Next?

Now that you have read through this book and learned how to make flashy, professional looking online presentations, you might be wondering what you should do next. Well, that depends on where you want to go. Are you happy with what you have learned, or do you want to further your knowledge with more advanced design applications?

If you do want to expand your knowledge, then you can look for some additional books on the software you wish to learn about. Focus on mastering the basics, and then apply what you have learned when going to more advanced material.

There are many great video resources as well, such as Pluralsight or CBT Nuggets, which offer online subscriptions to training videos of every type imaginable. YouTube is also a great source for instructional videos if you know what to search for.

If you are content with being a proficient Sway user that knows more than your friends, then just keep on practicing what you have learned. Don't be afraid to poke around with some of the features that you normally don't use and see if you can figure out what they do without having to research it since learning by doing is the most effective method to gain new skills.

Thanks for reading **Microsoft Sway Made Easy**. You can also check out the other books in the Made Easy series for additional computer related information and training. You can get more information on my other books on my Computers Made Easy Book Series website.

https://www.madeeasybookseries.com/

You should also check out my computer tips website, as well as follow it on Facebook to find more information on all kinds of computer topics.

www.onlinecomputertips.com
https://www.facebook.com/OnlineComputerTips/

About the Author

James Bernstein has been working with various companies in the IT field for over 20 years, managing technologies such as SAN and NAS storage, VMware, backups, Windows Servers, Active Directory, DNS, DHCP, Networking, Microsoft Office, Photoshop, Premiere, Exchange, and more.

He has obtained certifications from Microsoft, VMware, CompTIA, ShoreTel, and SNIA, and continues to strive to learn new technologies to further his knowledge on a variety of subjects.

He is also the founder of the website onlinecomputertips.com, which offers its readers valuable information on topics such as Windows, networking, hardware, software, and troubleshooting. James writes much of the content himself and adds new content on a regular basis. The site was started in 2005 and is still going strong today.

Printed in Great Britain
by Amazon

37418686R00053